My Grammar Dictionary

Name________________________________

Table of Contents

Parts of Speech Review 3-4

Appositives 5-6

Prepositional Phrases 7-8

Simple Sentences 9-10

Complete Subjects 11-12

Complete Predicates 13-14

Compound Sentences 15-16

Titles as Part of a Person's Name .17-18

Book Titles 19-20

Quotation Marks with Titles 21-22

Direct Quotations 23-24

Plural Possessives 25

Contractions 26-27

Abbreviations 28

End Punctuation 29-30

Commas 31-32

Parts of Speech Review

Noun

A noun is a general person, place, thing, or idea. A noun can be singular, plural, or possessive. Every sentence must have a noun.

1. The dog is barking.
2. The fastest students won.

Proper Noun

A proper noun is a specific person, place, or thing. Proper nouns are always capitalized.

1. I was born in the United States.
2. Her birthday is in August.

Pronoun

A pronoun takes the place of one or more nouns. An indefinite pronoun refers to an unnamed person or thing.

1. We are going to the store.
2. I hope everything is in order.

Adjective

An adjective is a word that modifies or describes a noun or pronoun.

1. The blue ball is lost.
2. The scary movie was hard to watch.

Proper Adjective

A proper adjective is an adjective that is formed from a proper noun. A proper adjective is always capitalized.

1. The Sunday newspaper has a comics section.
2. The Florida everglades are magnificent.

Parts of Speech Review

Verb
A verb tells what action a subject is performing. Every sentence must have a verb.

1. I <u>wrote</u> her a letter.
2. The cat <u>scratched</u> my arm.

Linking Verb
A linking verb links the subject with another word that renames or describes the subject. Forms of *be* are common linking verbs: *be*, *are*, *am*, *was*, *is*, and *were*.

1. December <u>is</u> a popular month for skiing.
2. The fur on the rabbit <u>feels</u> very soft.

Adverb
An adverb describes a verb, an adjective, or another adverb. In most cases an adverb is made by adding **ly** to an adjective.

1. The singer sang <u>softly</u> to us.
2. The crowd cheered <u>loudly</u>.

Preposition
A preposition shows the relationship between a noun or pronoun and another word in the sentence.

1. I can run five miles <u>with</u> ease.
2. The paper is <u>in</u> my desk.

Conjunction
A conjunction is used to connect words or groups of words.

1. Both red <u>and</u> green are holiday colors.
2. Will the teacher <u>or</u> the principal give the test?

Appositives

An appositive is a noun or pronoun that describes another noun or pronoun in a sentence.

The underlined word in each sentence is an appositive.

1. My sister, Lauren, is going to be five in June.
2. Illinois' capital, Springfield, is a beautiful place.
3. The substitute, Ms. Ryan, was very nice.
4. My dog, Luigi, is very friendly.
5. My favorite toy, a ship, was given to me by my best friend.
6. Our principal, Mr. Nelson, is planning to retire.
7. Joel, my neighbor's son, will be going to college next year.
8. Our state flower, the rose, comes in many colors.

More Examples:

Appositive Practice

Prepositional Phrases

A prepositional phrase is a group of words made up of a preposition, its object, and any words that describe the object. The prepositional phrase begins with a preposition and ends with a noun or pronoun.

The underlined words in each sentence are a prepositional phrase.

1. The brush was constantly dipped in the paint.
2. During the winter months, some animals hibernate.
3. The horse jumped over the railing.
4. I have been looking for those papers.
5. The soles of my shoes are worn out.
6. My friend was hiding behind the tree.

More Examples:

Prepositional Phrase Practice

Simple Sentences

A simple sentence has one subject and one verb. If two subjects share the same verb, or two verbs share the same subject, it is still a simple sentence.

The underlined words in each sentence are the subject. The words in ***bold*** *are the verbs.*

1. Tim and Alexandra **swam** together.
2. I **eat** fruit.
3. The printer and monitor **are** broken.
4. The house **is** cold and dark.
5. The ducks **quack** loudly.
6. That bird **bites**.
7. Baseball **is** fun.

More Examples:

Simple Sentence Practice

Complete Subjects

A complete subject includes all the words that are used to identify the person, place, thing, or idea the sentence is about.

The underlined portion in each sentence is the complete subject.

1. The large tree has many leaves.
2. Most children like to read.
3. My favorite show is on tonight.
4. The pool is large.
5. My baseball uniform is dirty.
6. The monkey ate a banana.
7. My computer is broken.
8. The bicycle has a flat tire.

More Examples:

Complete Subject Practice

Complete Predicates

A complete predicate includes all the words that explain what the subject is doing or explains something about the subject.

The underlined portion in each sentence is the complete predicate.

1. The rhinoceros has a sharp horn.
2. The flowers were drooping.
3. San Diego is a nice place to visit.
4. The speedboat won the race.
5. My favorite team won the championship.
6. The star is shining in the sky.
7. The skateboard championship is on Wednesday.
8. Our school is closed today.

More Examples:

Complete Predicate Practice

Compound Sentences

A compound sentence is made up of two simple sentences joined by a comma and a conjunction such as *and*, *but*, or *or*.

The underlined words are the first simple sentence in the compound sentence. The words in bold are the second simple sentence.

1. We were going to the game, but **it started to rain**.
2. I put money in the gumball machine, but **nothing came out**.
3. Juan rode his bike off the ramp, and **he lost control**.
4. Will you pay with cash, or **would you like to charge it**?
5. The baseball player hit the ball, and **he ran quickly to first base**.
6. I was going to write to you, but **I decided to call instead**.

More Examples:

____

____

____

____

____

____

Compound Sentence Practice

Titles as Part of a Person's Name

Capitalize titles that show office, rank, or profession when it comes before a person's name. Capitalize a title that shows a family relationship when it comes before a person's name.

The underlined word in each sentence is a title that should be capitalized.

1. I heard Queen Elizabeth is ill.
2. Grandma Jane is coming over today.
3. Vice President Gore made a speech.

Mr.	Congressman	Prince	Princess
Mrs.	President	Captain	Sergeant
Miss	Senator	Judge	General
Ms.	Governor	Colonel	Chief
Reverend	Mayor	Aunt	Councilman
Rabbi	Dr.	Uncle	

Title Practice

Book Titles

Capitalization
Capitalize the first word, last word, and all important words in the title of a book, newspaper, periodical, story, poem, movie, play, musical composition, or work of art.

Underlining
Underline the title of written works, musical works, titles of paintings, and names of vehicles.

The underlined words in each sentence must be capitalized and underlined.

1. I just read The Outsiders.
2. A Light in the Attic is a great poem.
3. Titanic was a blockbuster movie.
4. That new artist painted The Woods.
5. Here is your copy of US News and World Report.
6. The Client was written by John Grisham.
7. My father's favorite newspaper is the Chicago Tribune.
8. Do you know the words to Yankee Doodle?

Book Title Practice

Quotation Marks with Titles

Use quotation marks for the titles of chapters, articles, stories, plays, short poems, and songs.

The underlined words in each sentence must be in quotation marks.

1. "The Race" is the best chapter in the book.
2. My article, "Freedom," appeared in the New York Times.
3. "Jailhouse Rock" is a famous song by Elvis Presley.
4. "The Long Voyage Home" is a short play about sailors.
5. My sister wrote a short poem called, "Spring is Here."
6. My teacher asked us to read the chapter, "Voyage to the Moon."
7. My story, "How I Got My Cat," won the award.
8. My friend is starring in the play, "Summer Beach."

More Examples:

Quotation Marks with Title Practice

Direct Quotations

Use quotation marks to enclose someone's words. Do not use quotation marks when telling what someone else said without using the speaker's exact words.

The underlined words in the sentences must be enclosed in quotation marks.

1. I said, "You are late."
2. "Which shirt do you like most?" asked the salesgirl.
3. "Let me know when you are finished," said my teacher.
4. "Don't forget your lunch," dad shouted.
5. "You don't know what you are talking about," retorted Michele.

More Examples:

Direct Quotation Practice

Plural Possessives

Add *'s* to form the plural of a possessive noun that does not end in *s*. Add only an apostrophe to form the possessive of a plural noun that ends in *s*.

The underlined word in each sentence is a plural possessive.

1. The babies' blankets were new.
2. The librarians' books were reshelved.
3. The painters' brushes must be cleaned.

girls'	cars'	writers'	months'
teachers'	pigs'	students'	goats'
astronauts'	horses'	days'	roses'
nurses'	mens'	teams'	trees'
roads'	children's	sheep's	surgeons'
geese's	dolls'	friends'	women's

More Examples:

Contractions

A contraction is made when two words are put together. The apostrophe takes the place of one or more of the letters which have been taken away.

The underlined word in each sentence is a contraction.

1. He <u>isn't</u> going to ride his bike.
2. They <u>aren't</u> old enough yet.
3. He <u>can't</u> read that book.

I'll	I've	there's	it's
they're	he's	that's	you've
we'll	she's	here's	weren't
I'm	don't	he'd	we've
won't	wouldn't	she'd	didn't
let's	what's	you'd	couldn't

More Examples:

____________	____________	____________
____________	____________	____________
____________	____________	____________
____________	____________	____________
____________	____________	____________
____________	____________	____________

Apostrophe Practice

Abbreviations

An abbreviation is a shortened form of a word. Most abbreviations begin with a capital letter and end with a period.

The underlined word in each sentence is an abbreviation.

1. My dad goes to work in the P.M.
2. I live on Baker Dr.
3. Mr. Adams drove the car.

Blvd.	Wed.	Jan.	Esq.
A.M.	Mrs.	Mr.	Oct.
Mar.	Sen.	A.D.	yd.
St.	ft.	Dr.	V.P.
in.	Ave.	Ms.	Gov.
Sr.	Capt.	Fri.	lb.

More Examples:

End Punctuation

A **declarative** sentence makes a statement and ends in a period.

An **interrogative** sentence asks a question and ends with a question mark.

An **exclamatory** sentence expresses strong feelings or emotions and ends with an exclamation point.

Review the examples below.

Declarative:

1. It is time for school.
2. We are going to the movies.
3. You are my good friend.
4. That is my book.

More Examples:

______________________ ______________________

Interrogative:

1. Did you clean your room?
2. When is our vacation?
3. Where are my glasses?
4. What is her name?

More Examples:

______________________ ______________________

Exclamatory:

1. Let's go to the park now!
2. That was really good!
3. The house is on fire!
4. Come with me!

More Examples:

______________________ ______________________

End Punctuation Practice

Declarative:

Interrogative:

Exclamatory:

Commas

Commas in a Series
Three or more similar items together form a series. Use a comma to separate each item in the series.

Commas in Compound Sentences
Use a comma to separate the independent clauses of a compound sentence if the clauses are joined by a conjunction such as *and*, *but*, or *or*.

Commas After Introductions
Use a comma after certain introductory elements. Common introductory elements include *no*, *oh*, *well*, and *yes*.

Review the examples below.

Series

1. The drapes are brown, beige, and black.
2. I have one dime, two nickels, and three quarters.
3. Last summer we went to Colorado, Utah, and Nevada.

Compound Sentences.

1. Some bugs bite, but others sting.
2. You can stay here, or you can come home.
3. I dressed warmly for skiing, but I was still cold.

Introductions

1. Yes, you may come to my house.
2. No, the bike is not for sale.
3. Oh, what a great idea!

Comma Practice

Series:

Compound Sentences:

Introductions: